BRITISH RAILWAYS STEAMING IN THE MIDLANDS

Volume Two

Compiled by
PETER HANDS

DEFIANT PUBLICATIONS
190 Yoxall Road
Shirley, Solihull
West Midlands

Printed on behalf of Richard Netherwood Ltd., by Gorenjski tisk d.d., Slovenia

CURRENT STEAM PHOTOGRAPH ALBUMS AVAILABLE
FROM DEFIANT PUBLICATIONS

VOLUME 14
A4 size - Hardback. 96 pages
-178 b/w photographs.
£14.95 + £1.50 postage.
ISBN 0 946857 40 7.

VOLUME 15
A4 size - Hardback. 96 pages
-178 b/w photographs.
£16.95 + £1.50 postage.
ISBN 0 946857 52 0.

A 'VALEDICTION'
A4 size - Hardback. 96 pages
-173 b/w photographs.
£19.95 + £1.50 postage.
ISBN 0 946857 64 4.

VOLUME 1
A4 size - Hardback. 96 pages
-177 b/w photographs.
£14.95 + £1.50 postage.
ISBN 0 946857 41 5.

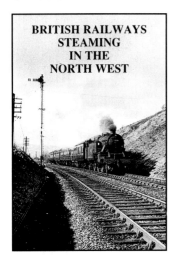

A4 size - Hardback. 96 pages
-174 b/w photographs.
£18.95 + £1.50 postage.
ISBN 0 946857 60 1

A4 size - Hardback. 96 pages
-177 b/w photographs.
£19.95 + £1.50 postage.
ISBN 0 946857 62 8.

VOLUME 11
A4 size - Hardback. 96 pages
-176 b/w photographs.
£16.95 + £1.50 postage.
ISBN 0 946857 48 2.

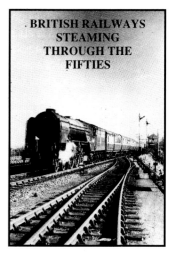

VOLUME 12
A4 size - Hardback. 96 pages
-176 b/w photographs.
£16.95 + £1.50 postage.
ISBN 0 946857 49 0.

VOLUME 1
A4 size - Hardback. 96 pages
-177 b/w photographs.
£14.95 + £1.50 postage.
ISBN 0 946857 39 3.

VOLUME 1
A4 size - Hardback. 96 pages
-174 b/w photographs.
£14.95 + £1.50 postage.
ISBN 0 946857 42 3.

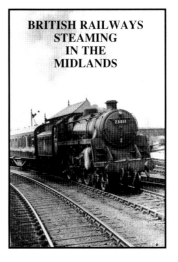

VOLUME 2
A4 size - Hardback. 96 pages
-177 b/w photographs.
£19.95 + £1.50 postage.
ISBN 0 946857 63 6.

VOLUME16
A4 size - Hardback. 96 pages
-178 b/w photographs.
£18.95 + £1.50 postage.
ISBN 0 946857 61 X

CURRENT STEAM PHOTOGRAPH ALBUMS
AVAILABLE AND OTHER TITLES

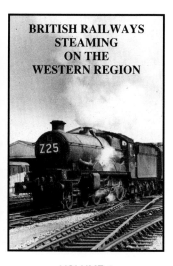

BRITISH RAILWAYS
STEAMING
ON THE
WESTERN REGION

VOLUME 4
A4 size - Hardback. 96 pages
-177 b/w photographs.
£15.95 + £1.50 postage.
ISBN 0 946857 46 6.

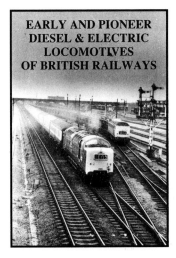

EARLY AND PIONEER
DIESEL & ELECTRIC
LOCOMOTIVES
OF BRITISH RAILWAYS

A4 size - Hardback. 96 pages
-177 b/w photographs.
£15.95 + £1.50 postage.
ISBN 0 946857 45 8.

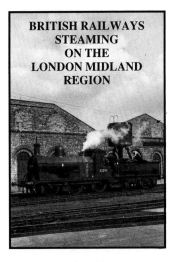

BRITISH RAILWAYS
STEAMING
ON THE
LONDON MIDLAND
REGION

VOLUME 4
A4 size - Hardback. 96 pages
-177 b/w photographs.
£15.95 + £1.50 postage.
ISBN 0 946857 47 4.

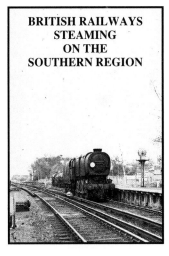

BRITISH RAILWAYS
STEAMING
ON THE
SOUTHERN REGION

VOLUME 3
A4 size - Hardback. 96 pages
-177 b/w photographs.
£17.95 + £1.50 postage.
ISBN 0 946857 54 7.

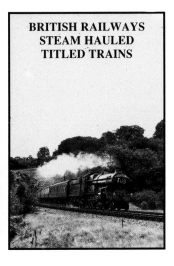

BRITISH RAILWAYS
STEAM HAULED
TITLED TRAINS

A4 size - Hardback. 96 pages
-169 b/w photographs.
£16.95 + £1.50 postage.
ISBN 0 946857 51 2.

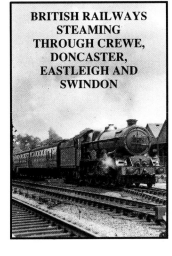

BRITISH RAILWAYS
STEAMING
THROUGH CREWE,
DONCASTER,
EASTLEIGH AND
SWINDON

A4 size - Hardback. 96 pages
-179 b/w photographs.
£17.95 + £1.50 postage.
ISBN 0 946857 53 9.

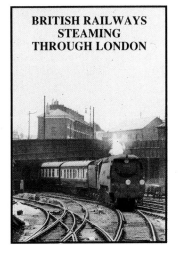

BRITISH RAILWAYS
STEAMING
THROUGH LONDON

A4 size - Hardback. 96 pages
-174 b/w photographs.
£17.95 + £1.50 postage.
ISBN 0 946857 55 5.

BRITISH RAILWAYS
STEAMING ON
THE EX-LNER
LINES

VOLUME 4
A4 size - Hardback. 96 pages
-183 b/w photographs.
£17.95 + £1.50 postage.
ISBN 0 946857 57 1.

BRITISH RAILWAYS
STEAMING FROM
1948–1968

'50th' ALBUM
A4 size - Hardback. 96 pages
-186 b/w photographs.
£16.95 + £1.50 postage.
ISBN 0 946857 50 4.

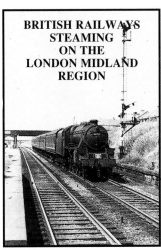

BRITISH RAILWAYS
STEAMING
ON THE
LONDON MIDLAND
REGION

VOLUME 5
A4 size - Hardback. 96 pages.
- 177 b/w photographs.
£17.95 + £1.50 postage.
ISBN 0 946857 58X.

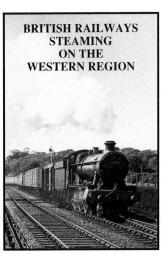

BRITISH RAILWAYS
STEAMING
ON THE
WESTERN REGION

VOLUME 5
A4 size - Hardback. 96 pages.
- 177 b/w photographs.
£17.95 + £1.50 postage.
ISBN 0 946857 59 8.

It's a dog's life in the
FIRE SERVICE
by Peter St.Bernard

COMEDY
269 pages. Cartoons.
£9.95 + £1.00 postage.
ISBN 0 946857 30 X.

ACKNOWLEDGEMENTS

Grateful thanks are extended to the following contributors of photographs not only for their use in this book but for their kind patience and long term loan of negatives/photographs whilst this book was being compiled.

T.R.AMOS	P.A.BRIDGMAN	B.W.L.BROOKSBANK
TAMWORTH	HUCCLECOTE	MORDEN
N.L.BROWNE	R.S.CARPENTER	KEN ELLIS
ALDERSHOT	BIRMINGHAM	SWINDON
A.N.H.GLOVER	J.D.GOMERSALL	A.E GOULDING
BIRMINGHAM	SHEFFIELD	TRURO
B.K.B.GREEN	PETER HAY	R.W.HINTON
WARRINGTON	HOVE	GLOUCESTER
I.J.HODSON	J.JAMES	G.JINKS
CAMBRIDGE	IPSWICH	BIRMINGHAM
D.K.JONES	ERIC LIGHT	R.PICTON
MOUNTAIN ASH	TICKHILL	WOLVERHAMPTON
N.E.PREEDY	P.A.ROWLINGS	J.SCHATZ
GLOUCESTER	ALCONBURY	LITTLETHORPE
C.P.STACEY	TERRY WARD	D.WEBSTER
STONY STRATFORD	NORTHAMPTON	*
KIT WINDLE	MIKE WOOD	N.WOOD
LOWER BREDBURY	BIRMINGHAM	DERBY

* Courtesy of the Norman Preedy collection.

Front Cover - With a clear road ahead, BR Class 5 4-6-0 No 73011, looking fresh from overhaul, leaves Gloucester (Eastgate) station with a Bristol (Temple Meads) to Sheffield (Midland) stopping train in March 1957. The depot plate indicates that No 73011 was an inmate of 19B Millhouses. Later in life, prior to withdrawal in November 1967, No 73011 was also allocated to 6J Holyhead, 6G Llandudno Junction, 1G Woodford Halse, 2B Oxley and 9H Patricroft. (N.E.Preedy)

ISBN 0 946857 63 6

(C) P.B.HANDS 1998
FIRST PUBLISHED 1998

INTRODUCTION

BRITISH RAILWAYS STEAMING THROUGH THE MIDLANDS - Volume Two is the second such album to cover this important area of England in both industrial and rural terms.

The author hopes the reader will enjoy the wide variety of locations and motive power included in this album. Almost seventy different venues have been included involving the work of twenty-seven photographers. Some areas of greater interest, such as Birmingham, Crewe, Derby, Gloucester, Oxford, Rugby, Shrewsbury, Walsall and Worcester have been given more coverage than others.

It is hoped that the reader will appreciate that it is difficult to pinpoint the dividing lines between what constitutes the exact geographical area of the Midlands.

The 'BR Steaming' series of books are designed to give the ordinary, everyday steam photographic enthusiast of the 1950's and 1960's a chance to participate in and give pleasure to others whilst recapturing the twilight days of steam.

The majority of the photographs used in this album have been contributed by readers of Peter Hands series of booklets entitled 'What Happened To Steam' & 'BR Steam Shed Allocations' (both still available) and from readers of the earlier 'BR Steaming Through The Sixties' albums. In normal circumstances these may have been hidden from the public eye for ever.

Where possible, no famous names will be found in this album, nor will photographs which have been published before be used. Nevertheless, the content and quality of photographs used are second to none.

If you require any further information about the availability of the books in the 'Defiant Publications' range, please contact:

Tel. No.
0121 745-8421

Peter Hands,
190 Yoxall Road,
Shirley, Solihull,
West Midlands B90 3RN

CONTENTS

MEMORIES OF THE MIDLANDS

1) Newland Halt, facing Worcester in 1960. (R.S.Carpenter)

2) Wednesbury station, ex.GWR in 1957. (R.S.Carpenter)

3) Overseal sub-shed on 14th June 1959. (R.S.Carpenter)

4) Buxton M.P.D. coaling plant on 27.3.67. (N.Wood)

5) 16B Colwick in May 1966. (C.P.Stacey)

6) The driver of recently outshopped Riddles WD Class 8F 2-8-0 No 90507, of 38E Woodford Halse, gives his attention to the driving wheels of his charge from the platform at Grange Court Junction, near Gloucester in the winter of 1957. No 90507, in charge of a Class 8 loose-coupled freight, was transferred northwards to 8F Springs Branch Wigan in March 1959. Condemned in July 1963 from 8F, No 90507 was cut up at Crewe Works two months later. (R.W.Hinton)

7) Up until the end of 1962, when the class was rendered extinct, the LNER L1 2-6-4 Tanks were a common sight on the former Great Central main line on suburban trains. Approaching Rugby GC station, in sunlight and shadow, No 67799, of 40E Colwick, steams beneath a road bridge with a southbound local in the late fifties. Introduced into service in 1945, the 100 units of this robust class were allocated to depots as far apart as Norwich and Darlington. (R.S.Carpenter)

8) A packed yard at 17A Derby on 12th April 1953. The main focus of the photographer's attention is LMS Class 5 4-6-0 No 44986 which is coupled to a self-weighing tender. During its latter years of service, No 44986 was allocated to 19B Millhouses, 6J Holyhead, 8B Warrington, 6B Mold Junction and 12A Carlisle (Kingmoor). Alongside No 44986 is LMS Class 4F 0-6-0 No 44270 which was taken out of revenue earning service from 16A Toton in November 1963. (B.K.B.Green)

9) With an unidentified GWR 5101 Class 2-6-2T in the background, GWR *Hall* Class 4-6-0 No 6916 *Misterton Hall*, from 85C Hereford, is almost ready to depart from platform three at Birmingham (Snow Hill) with a semi-fast in March 1957. Three months on and *Misterton Hall* was on the move to a new home at 84G Shrewsbury where it remained until June 1964. Its last abode was at 2D Banbury. After withdrawal in August 1965 it was cut up on site at the depot. (R.S.Carpenter)

10) Paintwork gleaming and looking fresh from overhaul at Crewe Works, LMS Unrebuilt *Patriot* Class 4-6-0 No 45524 *Blackpool*, of 12A Carlisle (Upperby), waits in a centre road at Shrewsbury to take over a northbound excursion on a sun-filled 3rd June 1952. Standing alongside *Blackpool* is 84A Wolverhampton (Stafford Road) based GWR *Castle* Class 4-6-0 No 5022 *Wigmore Castle* with a down express. *Blackpool* was condemned from 8A Edge Hill (Liverpool) in September 1962. (B.K.B.Green)

11) Its tender filled to the brim with coal supplies, GWR *Castle* Class 4-6-0 No 5033 *Broughton Castle* simmers gently on the turntable at 81F Oxford in July 1959 shortly after being transferred to the shed from 84K Chester GWR. Destined to remain at Oxford for the rest of its working life, *Broughton Castle*, like *Blackpool* in the previous frame, was condemned during the great slaughter of steam in September 1962 after covering 1,150,197 miles. (R.S.Carpenter)

12) The massive freight orientated depot at Toton, situated between Stapleford & Sandiacre and Long Eaton stations, housed a huge allocation of steam locomotives including a legion of LMS 0-6-0 types used in the main on mineral trains and pick-up freights to and from the Nottingham area. On 13th May 1956, 4F No 43900, a visitor to Toton from 18D Staveley (Barrow Hill), is seen at rest in the yard in the company of an unidentified Class 3F 0-6-0. (B.K.B.Green)

13) Looking in respectable external condition, locally based LMS Class 6P5F 'Crab' Class 2-6-0 No 42791 is stabled out of steam in the yard at 21A Saltley next to an unidentified BR Class 9F 2-10-0 in March 1956. No 42790 was drafted to the Manchester area in June 1961 being allocated to 9G Gorton. In the left of the picture we can just make out the cab and part of the tender of former MR Class 3F 0-6-0 No 43684 which was withdrawn from 21A in June 1957. (N.E.Preedy)

14) Having almost breasted the summit at Hatton, GWR 5101 Class 2-6-2T No 4112, from 84D Leamington, steams through the station and heads for Lapworth light engine on a gloomy 4th September 1960. Until the advent of colour-light signalling in the area, Hatton boasted three signalboxes - North, South and West. The author was based at the West box (Class 4) from October 1964 until February 1965, before moving to a Class 3 box at Earlswood Lakes station. (D.K.Jones)

15) A legion of Riddles War Department Class 8F 2-8-0's were based at Woodford Halse shed, coded 38E, 2G, 2F and 1G in BR days and all were employed on freight workings on the former Great Central main line. On an unknown date in 1952, No 90520 belches out black smoke as it heads an up goods through Woodford Halse station. Between December 1963 and withdrawal in February 1965, No 90520 was reallocated to 16A Toton, 9D Newton Heath and 8L Aintree. (R.S.Carpenter)

16) The Midland Railway Class 2P 4-4-0's, series Nos 40400-40562 designed by Johnson, introduced into service between 1891-1901 were later rebuilt by Fowler (1912-1923). These handsome locos were a product of the Midland Railway 'small engine policy' and were employed for many years on expresses. In their latter years they were mostly confined to local passenger, freight and pilot duties. No 40556 is seen here in the shed yard at 18C Hasland on 8th July 1951. (B.K.B.Green)

17) The driver and fireman of BR Class 5 4-6-0 No 73013 (84K Chester GWR) combine to supply their charge with refreshment from the near at hand water column near to the now long-gone turntable at the Wolverhampton end of Birmingham (Snow Hill) in September 1957. In the left of the frame is an unidentified GWR *Modified Hall* Class 4-6-0. No 73013 later served from the sheds at 6A Chester (LMR), 1A Willesden, 1E Bletchley, 2B Oxley, 2D Banbury and 9K Bolton. (R.S.Carpenter)

18) Based at 3A Bescot (the abandoned steam running shed is still intact today) LMS Class 8F 2-8-0 No 48477 leaves a trail of black fumes as it passes through Walsall with lengthy southbound empties in 1956. Shortly before closure to steam in March 1966, No 48477 was transferred from Bescot to 2A Tyseley where it was little used up until condemnation seven months later. Four months after withdrawal it was cut up at Cashmores yard in Great Bridge. (R.S.Carpenter)

19) Less than eleven years of age, GWR *Castle* Class 4-6-0 No 5077 *Fairey Battle* stands near to Cheltenham Spa Malvern Road West Signal Box prior to departing with an express on 29th May 1949. No 5077, originally named *Eastnor Castle* (a name later carried by No 7004), was renamed *Fairey Battle* in October 1940. During its latter years of service, No 5077 worked from the sheds at 87E Landore (Swansea) and 87F Llanelly. It was withdrawn from 87F in July 1962. (R.S.Carpenter)

20) The former Great Central Railway Robinson inspired 2-8-0's had a long association with the shed at Colwick, coded 38A, 40E and 16B during BR times, but by Sunday 25th July 1965 their active ranks had been reduced to a handful, one being begrimed 04/7 Class No 63770 seen in steam in the yard. Once of 40B Immingham, No 63770 had been allocated to Colwick since December 1958. Condemned from Colwick in December 1965 it was scrapped three months later. (N.Wood)

21) With the safety valves lifting from a sister engine in the left of the frame and a GWR 57xx Class 0-6-0PT lurking in the background, locally based GWR 5101 Class 2-6-2T No 5166 poses for the camera in the shed yard at 84E Tyseley in September 1957 a month before being drafted to 86E Severn Tunnel Junction. At the latter shed No 5166 worked out its final years of service mainly on pilot duties through the Severn tunnel prior to withdrawal in May 1961. (R.S.Carpenter)

22) With a member of the footplate crew in attendance, ex.works LMS *Jubilee* Class 4-6-0 No 45598 *Basutoland*, from 14B Kentish Town and paired with a smaller capacity Fowler tender, is prepared for action over an ashpit at 5A Crewe (North) on 1st August 1952. *Basutoland* remained on the books at Kentish Town until November 1959, moving to 17A Derby. Two years later and it was on the move again, this time to 17B Burton. 8K Bank Hall was its last abode. (B.K.B.Green)

23) The sun's rays reflect off the boiler of LMS *Royal Scot* Class 4-6-0 No 46159 *The Royal Air Force*, a 5A Crewe (North) steed, as a strong wind blows excess steam and smoke sidewards at Birmingham (New Street) as it awaits departure with an express in the mid-fifties. *The Royal Air Force* remained on top-link passenger duties from 5A until despatched to 1A Willesden in January 1961. It eked out its final days at 1A until withdrawn in November 1962. (R.S.Carpenter)

24) From the end of 1965 steam was very much in retreat in the Derby area and the sight of 50A York based WD Class 8F 2-8-0 No 90078 was very much a rarity by the middle of 1966. With the footplate crew leaning out of the cab, No 90078 approaches Derby, London Road with a Class 8 loose-coupled freight. Ousted from York shed in October 1966, No 90078 had a new, but very brief, lease of life at 52G Sunderland, being taken out of service the following month. (N.Wood)

25) Leaving a trail of black exhaust fumes in its wake, GWR 5700 Class 0-6-0PT No 9640 (2B Oxley) rattles towards the photographer at Wednesbury (GWR) with a train of flats on 18th April 1964. By this date the former WR lines in the Midlands were firmly in the grip of the LMR authorities who were probably already plotting the demise of the former GWR route from Wolverhampton (Low Level) to Birmingham (Snow Hill), which they succeeded in shutting down on 4th March 1972. (T.R.Amos)

26) LNER B16/3 Class 4-6-0 No 61463, from 50A York, speeds southwards with a vacuum-fitted freight near to Rugby GC in the late fifties. The B16/3's, with a power classification of 5MT, originally designed by Raven, were later rebuilt by Thompson (1944) and the B16's as a whole were the last example of Raven designed passenger engines to survive into the latter days of steam. The final survivors were withdrawn from service by July 1964. (R.S.Carpenter)

27) A vertical plume of smoke from the funnel of a rather less than clean WD Class 8F 2-8-0 No 90295 informs us it is alive and well inside the whitewashed walls of the roundhouse at 41E Staveley (Barrow Hill) on 25th July 1965. For many years a 24C Lostock Hall and 24B Rose Grove steed, No 90295 had been transferred to the Eastern Region shed at Barrow Hill a month before this picture was taken. By October 1965 it was based at 40E Colwick. (N.Wood)

28) Two youngsters pose proudly for the camera inside the cab of LMS *Jubilee* Class 4-6-0 No 45640 *Frobisher* which is hemmed between a bufferstop and a wagon in the yard of its home depot at 16A Nottingham on 22nd June 1952. Years later *Frobisher* found its way to the Scottish Region at 68A Carlisle (Kingmoor) which was taken over by the LMR in February 1958, becoming 12A. *Frobisher* continued to work out of Kingmoor shed until withdrawn in March 1964. (B.K.B.Green)

29) Most Western Region orientated locomotives were serviced at Gresty Lane shed when visiting Crewe, but on 6th September 1961 GWR *Hall* Class 4-6-0 No 4912 *Berrington Hall* has had its needs attended to at 5B Crewe (South). It is seen here ready to depart from the yard, its tender filled with coal. Once of 84A Wolverhampton (Stafford Road) and 84G Shrewsbury, *Berrington Hall* had been at Oxley since April 1959. It was withdrawn from the same in August 1962. (R.S.Carpenter)

30) With the driver on the footplate and the fireman replenishing his water supply, GWR *Grange* Class 4-6-0 No 6876 *Kingsland Grange*, of 86A Newport (Ebbw Junction), waits impatiently for the off at Hereford (Barrs Court) station with a fitted freight in September 1959. *Kingsland Grange* had been an Ebbw Junction engine since moving from 82B St.Philip's Marsh in April 1959. Between June 1964 and withdrawal in November 1965 it was subjected to four more transfers. (R.S.Carpenter)

31) 2B Oxley based LMS Class 5 4-6-0 No 45283 leaves Gloucester and blasts towards Midland Road foot crossing with the 9.30am Saturdays Only Wolverhampton (Low Level) to Paignton express packed with expectant holidaymakers. Today there is no sign of the railway in this location with the trackbed now part of the inner ring road in Gloucester. No 45283 had made its way to Oxley in April 1965 by way of the sheds at Shrewsbury, Mold Junction and Saltley. (N.E.Preedy)

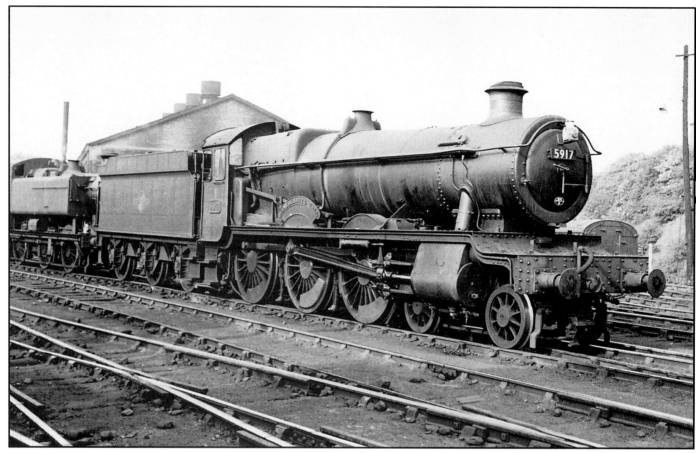

32) With an unidentified GWR 9400 Class heavy shunter 0-6-0PT bringing up the rear, locally based GWR *Hall* Class 4-6-0 No 5917 *Westminster Hall* awaits its next rostered turn in the yard at 85A Worcester in the summer of 1962. The end is on the horizon for *Westminster Hall* with condemnation looming in September of the same year. Consisting of two separate structures, Worcester shed was situated in a triangle between Shrub Hill, Rainbow Hill and Tunnel Junctions. (D.K.Jones)

33) Another locomotive in its death throes in 1962, a disastrous year for steam withdrawals, was LNER L1 Class 2-6-4T No 67746 (40E Colwick) seen here backing towards some coaching stock at Derby (Friargate) station in the winter of the same. Friargate station, of Great Northern Railway origin, closed during 1964. No 67746, once of 34D Hitchin and 34A Kings Cross, was taken out of revenue earning service in July 1962 and scrapped at Darlington Works. (R.S.Carpenter)

34) A soaking wet day at Crewe station on 28th November 1964 where BR *Britannia* Class 4-6-2 No 70052 *Firth of Tay*, from the nearby North shed (5A), is employed on a Warwickshire Railway Society special from Birmingham (New Street) to Carlisle (Citadel). It is nice to report that this Society is still active today, catering for the needs of enthusiasts who enjoy both UK and continental railways. If only the same could be said for the now long-gone No 70052. (G.Jinks)

35) A bright spring day at Uttoxeter where a smartly turned-out LMS Class 4F 0-6-0 No 44363 is a visitor to the shed (5F) from 5D Stoke on 12th April 1958. Two months on and No 44363 was destined to be a long-term resident at Crewe Works, where, after withdrawal in December 1963, it was cut up at the same. Uttoxeter shed, once belonging to the North Staffordshire Railway, only ever had a small allocation and closed its doors for ever on 7th December 1964. (R.S.Carpenter)

36) Nostalgia-time at 3A Bescot - circa 1957, where a lengthy line of freight engines stabled in the yard include at least three former London & North Western Class 7F 0-8-0's. Nearest the camera is No 48950, its basically designed tender filled with a more than ample coal supply in readiness for its next day of work. An inmate of Bescot, No 48950 was later transferred to a final home at 3B Bushbury (Wolverhampton) from whence it was withdrawn in December 1961. (N.E.Preedy)

37) A Scotsman, hands behind his back and complete with the kilt of his Clan, puffs away on a cigarette as he studies the presence of January 1937 constructed GWR *Grange* Class 4-6-0 No 6821 *Leaton Grange* at Oxford station on 26th August 1959. This locally based engine (81F) has been entrusted with an express bound for Paddington. Once of 83D Laira (Plymouth), No 6821 had been at Oxford shed since March 1958. It was condemned from 87F Llanelly in November 1964. (N.L.Browne)

38) The weeds are beginning to take over one of the island platforms at Small Heath & Sparkbrook as LMS Class 5 4-6-0 No 44860 (2D Banbury) lays a smokescreen as it steams through the station with an up fitted freight in August 1966. By this stage in time steam was very much in retreat in the West Midlands and sights like this were soon to become a thing of the past. No 44860, a Rugby engine for many years was transferred to 5D Stoke in September 1966. (N.Wood)

39) In days gone by, find a gasometer in a town and the chances were there would be a steam depot close at hand. This was the case at Gloucester where Horton Road (85B) once existed. As weeds began to take over the tracks in the yard, GWR 4300 Class 2-6-0 No 6394 is seen in steam in the company of a Hymeck Class Diesel, No D7052 on a sun-filled 26th July 1963. Both are long gone, No 6394 from 85B in June 1964 and No D7052 from Cardiff (Canton) in October 1972. (N.E.Preedy)

40) With a partially clear road ahead the driver of GWR *Modified Hall* Class 4-6-0 No 7918 *Rhose Wood Hall* has shut off steam as his charge approaches Kidderminster with a Birmingham (Snow Hill) to Hereford local passenger on a dull day in 1964. Today, Kidderminster (BR) still has a manual signalbox, albeit with London Midland Region upper quadrant signals instead of the former GWR types which abound at the adjacent Severn Valley Railway terminus. (R.S.Carpenter)

41) Looking somewhat bedraggled, LMS *Coronation* Class 4-6-2 No 46246 *City of Manchester*, of 5A Crewe (North), stands at Shrewsbury station in 1952. Constructed at Crewe Works at the height of the Second World War in 1943, *City of Manchester* was originally streamlined. Reallocated to 1B Camden in June 1960, No 46246 was withdrawn in January 1963. The last time the author saw it in action was at Birmingham (New Street) with an express in March 1962. (R.S.Carpenter)

42) A packed yard at 21A Saltley on an overcast 17th February 1962. In the foreground, in the company of two unidentified LMS Class 5 4-6-0's, is work-stained LMS Class 8F 2-8-0 No 48718, a visitor to 21A from 21D Aston. To the left of No 48718 is locally based LMS Class 5 4-6-0 No 44945. Both locomotives remained in the Midlands area until rendered redundant - No 48718 from 5E Nuneaton in April 1966 and No 44945 from 2B Oxley six months later. (R.S.Carpenter)

43) Shortly after changing shedcodes from 84E to 2A, Tyseley based BR Class 9F 2-10-0 No 92212 is noted in light steam in the large shed yard at 2B Oxley on a dull 29th October 1963. Released into revenue earning traffic at 84C Banbury in September 1959, No 92212 had spells at 82F Bath Green Park and 86A Newport (Ebbw Junction) before joining the books at Tyseley in July 1962. Withdrawn in January 1968 it is now back in service at the Great Central Railway. (P.A.Rowlings)

44) This candid snapshot shows the typical stance of the veteran steam man on the footplate over a quarter of a century ago. The driver of LMS Class 5 4-6-0 No 44804, from 21A Saltley, takes a breather at Derby station on Saturday, 9th June 1962. No 44804 took its leave of Saltley shed in May 1963, moving to 15C Leicester (Midland). Six months later and No 44804 was on the move to 16C Derby. A final transfer in July 1965 took it to 9E Trafford Park. (J.D.Gomersall)

45) With the driver oiling the motion and his fireman leaning out of the cab, a hard-working member of the shed staff at Kettering tops up the tender of 8H Birkenhead based LMS Class 9F 2-10-0 No 92089 with supplies from the patched-up coaling stage on 15th May 1965, a month before the depot closed completely. No 92089, built in September 1956 and withdrawn in February 1967, also worked from the depots at Doncaster, Annesley, Leicester (Midland) and Speke Junction. (D.Webster)

46) GWR *Castle* Class 4-6-0 No 5026 *Criccieth Castle*, sports the special headcode *X03* as it bursts beneath a bridge and heads towards Wednesbury (Hill Tip) tunnel with an excursion on 30th December 1958. *Criccieth Castle*, drafted to 84A Wolverhampton (Stafford Road) from 81F Oxford earlier in the year, later acquired a double chimney (October 1959). Upon the closure of Stafford Road in September 1963, No 5026 moved to 2B Oxley where it survived until November 1964. (T.R.Amos)

47) Outshopped at Crewe Works on 20th August 1955, BR *Britannia* Class 4-6-2 No 70015 *Apollo* (81A Old Oak Common) is accompanied by LMS Class 5 4-6-0 No 45386 and L & Y Class 3F 0-6-0 No 52507. During its short working life (sixteen years), *Apollo* was also allocated to 1B Camden, 30A Stratford, 86C Cardiff (Canton), 9E Trafford Park, 26A Newton Heath, 14D Neasden, 16D Annesley, 1A Willesden, 5A Crewe (North), 9B Stockport and 12A Carlisle (Kingmoor). (R.S.Carpenter)

48) Looking in fine external fettle, LMS Class 3 2-6-2T No 40146 (allocation unknown) is coaled and ready for its next duty in the depot yard at 2B Nuneaton on a sunny 4th July 1952. Records show us that later in life, No 40146 was allocated to 16C Mansfield from January 1957 until the closure of the same in April 1960. It then moved the short distance to 16B Kirby-in-Ashfield where it was destined to die in August 1962. Scrapping occurred in April 1963. (A.N.H.Glover)

49) Built by Neilson and Company in 1876 as pre-BR No 2996, Johnson former Midland Railway Class 2F 0-6-0 No 58169, shedded locally at 3C, blows off excess steam as it is photographed at Walsall station during the mid-fifties with a pick-up freight. The soot-stained station canopy in the background is in dire need of a fresh coat of paint to brush up its image. When Walsall shed closed to steam in June 1958, No 58169 found a new abode at 3B Bescot. (R.S.Carpenter)

50) Fresh from overhaul at Swindon Works and sporting a new double chimney, GWR *Castle* Class 4-6-0 No 7002 *Devizes Castle*, from 85A Worcester, has a clear road ahead as it speeds past the small signalbox at Naas Crossing, near Haresfield, with the heavily loaded 1.45pm express from Paddington to Gloucester and Cheltenham Spa on 29th July 1961. Destined for condemnation from Worcester in March 1964, No 7002 was scrapped at Cashmores, Great Bridge. (B.W.L.Brooksbank)

51) With the sun's rays reflecting off the clouds of smoke, the Worcestershire countryside reverberates to the cacophony of noise coming from the toils of LMS *Jubilee* Class 4-6-0 No 45597 *Barbados*, from 55A Leeds (Holbeck), and the Bromsgrove based banking engine as they attack the formidable Lickey incline with a northbound express on 16th April 1955. *Barbados*, for many years a favourite at Holbeck shed, was withdrawn from there in January 1965. (R.S.Carpenter)

52) Once of 6G Llandudno Junction, 21D Aston, 6J Holyhead and Llandudno Junction (again), LMS Class 5 4-6-0 No 44865 found itself at 1A Willesden from February to September 1965 and on 25th July 1965 it was a visitor to 16B Annesley where it is seen with its front end covered in discarded ash in front of the running shed. To gain access to Annesley shed one had to cross Newstead colliery yard and at night the overhead swinging buckets were an eerie sound. (N.Wood)

53) The two white lamps affixed to the front bufferbeam of GWR *Modified Hall* Class 4-6-0 No 7912 *Little Linford Hall* makes the external condition of this locomotive even worse than it probably is as it stands in steam in the yard of its home shed at 2D Banbury on a damp 31st May 1964. Of the seventy-one members of the class, seven are either preserved or awaiting restoration today, these being Nos 6960, 6984, 6989, 6990, 6998, 7903 and 7927. (Terry Ward)

54) The shocking state of the next locomotive featured makes *Little Linford Hall* look fresh from Swindon Works in comparision. BR *Britannia* Class 4-6-2 No 70031 *Byron*, of 21D Aston, passes the giant AEI complex at Rugby on the West Coast Main Line with an express on 20th July 1962. Released into traffic in November 1952, *Byron* spent most of its working life at sheds associated directly or indirectly with the WCML. It was withdrawn in November 1967. (D.K.Jones)

55) Pure white smoke engulfs the railway scene at Wednesbury as work-stained LMS Class 8F 2-8-0 No 48101 (2F Bescot) ploughs towards the camera with a train of flats on 13th April 1964. Transferred to 21A Saltley in February 1959 from 16B Kirby-in-Ashfield, No 48101 remained a firm favourite at the depot until being despatched to Bescot in March 1964. It returned to Saltley again for a final stint in December 1965 and was condemned in September 1966. (T.R.Amos)

56) On the very subject of Bescot shed, we find ourselves in the yard of the same on 12th April 1963 where LMS Class 5 4-6-0 No 45332 is a visitor from 8C Speke Junction. To the right of this engine is a former Ministry of Supply mineral wagon. Prior to being allocated to 8C in September 1962, from January 1957 onwards No 45332 worked from the sheds at Preston, Northampton, Aston, Bushbury and Chester. It died at Speke shed in November 1966. (R.S.Carpenter)

57) In the company of a GWR 2-6-2T type, War Department Class 8F 2-8-0 No 90483 stands out of steam in an almost deserted yard at 84D Leamington on 29th June 1952. This compact depot, a fifteen minute walk from the General station, was the first of the Churchward standard straight sheds to be constructed for the GWR (1906). It had four roads, a turntable and a coaling stage with a 45,000 gallon tank on top. Recoded 2L in September 1963 it closed in June 1965. (D.K.Jones)

58) The fireman of GWR *Manor* Class 4-6-0 No 7818 *Granville Manor* (withdrawn from 6F Machynlleth in January 1965) looks towards the camera prior to his charge departing with a morning local passenger train from Cirencester (Watermoor) in the mid-fifties. Watermoor station, of Midland and South Western Junction Railway origin, was destined for closure in 1961. Cirencester's remaining rail link from the Town station (GWR) to Kemble was severed during 1964. (R.S.Carpenter)

59) From far-off 86C Cardiff (Canton), WD Class 8F 2-8-0 No 90201 rattles past a signalbox at Woodford Halse with an immense rake of down mineral wagons in 1957. A large number of these engines, nicknamed 'bed-irons' by many spotters, were based on the Western Region, but all were either withdrawn or transferred away from the region by December 1962. After brief spells at 81E Didcot and 86A Newport (Ebbw Junction), No 90201 was drafted to 9G Gorton in July 1962. (R.S.Carpenter)

60) Beyer-Garratt 2-6-6-2T No 47967 (18A Toton) belches out black smoke as it clambers up the stiff grade after passing Birmingham City Football Club with a Gloucester bound freight at Bordesley Junction in the early fifties. Although this junction still exists today, No 47967 is long gone (November 1957) along with the signalbox, semaphore signals and cattle wagons. Even the bus depot in the background, although still in situ, has been closed for many years. (R.S.Carpenter)

61) Despite the fact that in excess of three years have passed by since the old London Midland and Scottish Railway was rendered defunct, LMS *Royal Scot* Class 4-6-0 No 46111 *Royal Fusilier*, of 8A Edge Hill (Liverpool), still sports LMS on its tender as it rests in weak sunshine in the yard at 5A Crewe (North) on 4th February 1951. A regular performer on the WCML, No 46111 lost its links with the same when it was drafted to 16D Annesley in January 1963. (B.K.B.Green)

62) Two deserted roads inside one of the two roundhouses at Tyseley shed on 24th September 1963 has allowed enough room for the photographer to capture this three-quarter shot of locally based GWR *Hall* Class 4-6-0 No 5988 *Bostock Hall*. Up until March 1960, when it was reallocated to 84C Banbury, *Bostock Hall* was very much a rarity in the Midlands, previously being shedded at 87E Landore (Swansea). Its days of steaming came to an end in October 1965. (Mike Wood)

63) The photographer must have been on the brink of falling out of his carriage window as he obtained this impressive picture of LMS Class 5 4-6-0 No 44831, from 5E Nuneaton, as it blasted out of Uttoxeter station with a Derby (Midland) to Llandudno express in the summer of 1965. Once of the sheds at Rugby and Stoke, No 44831 also served from the ones at Holyhead, Chester and Springs Branch Wigan before being taken out of revenue earning service in November 1967. (N.Wood)

64) BR Class 9F 2-10-0 No 92150, an inhabitant of 2E Saltley, crosses the Gloucester avoiding line with a Class 8 loose-fitted freight bound for Bristol on a bright 20th September 1964. This modern locomotive was destined for an all too brief life span of only ten years thanks to the shortsighted mandarins within the 'rush to modernise' think tank. A Saltley loco for much of its career, No 92150 was also based at 18B Westhouses, 2A Tyseley and 56A Wakefield. (N.E.Preedy)

65) From the 'mighty' we switch to the 'humble', where, crowded on the small footplate of LMS Class 0F 0-4-0ST No 41523, with its spartan protection against the elements, are three 'posing' members of the railway fraternity. No 41523, of late 1890's vintage, is seen at Burton-on-Trent on 19th August 1951. With its 3'10" driving wheels it was ideal for use on the tight curves of the myriad of lines which once served the host of breweries in the Burton area. (B.K.B.Green)

66) LNER J39 Class 0-6-0 No 64984, allocation not known, is a 'stranger-in-the-camp, as it gleams in the fierce summer sunshine in the shed yard at 17A Derby on 19th August 1951 after being outshopped from the nearby works complex after heavy repair. The J39's, designed by Gresley, were not affected by withdrawals until 1959 when forty-eight of their number were condemned, including No 64984, which was scrapped at Stratford Works in January 1960. (N.E.Preedy)

67) LMS Class 8F 2-8-0 No 48538, from 16G Westhouses, rests in the yard at 15C Kettering after working a special freight to the area on 27th March 1965. From January 1957 onwards No 48538 also worked from the sheds at Toton, Cricklewood, Colwick and Saltley before its days of 'glory' came to an end in March 1967. Alongside No 48538 is LMS *Jubilee* Class 4-6-0 No 45573 *Newfoundland*, from 55A Leeds (Holbeck), which was withdrawn from the same in September 1965. (D.Webster)

68) With its lengthy train of vans snaking behind, BR *Britannia* Class 4-6-2 No 70049 *Solway Firth*, of 12A Carlisle (Kingmoor) and denuded of nameplates, drifts into Crewe station with an up parcels on 22nd July 1967. Placed into service in July 1954 at 6J Holyhead it was to be almost five years before some 'Brain of Britain' within the BR hierarchy conjured up the name *'Solway Firth'* for No 70049, which spent all of its working life based at MPD's on the LMR. (N.Wood)

69) The 41xx and 51xx series of GWR 2-6-2 Tanks were a common sight on Western Region tracks in the Midlands, but not so their counterparts from the 61xx series, most of which worked in and around London (Paddington) on suburban duties. One exception was No 6139, from 84E Tyseley, seen here at Birmingham (Snow Hill) on an empty stock train in 1958. In March 1960 Tyseley shed lost the services of No 6139 when it was transferred southwards to 81F Oxford. (R.S.Carpenter)

70) The LMS Ivatt 'Flying Pig' Class 2-6-0's were ungainly looking locomotives at the best of times, but when fitted with a stovepipe chimney it made them look ridiculous as can be seen with No 43027, complete with a 'posing crew', at Rubery on 11th April 1951 on pick-up duties from Washwood Heath Sidings. No 43027 (equipped later with a conventional chimney) served from a host of sheds, including Derby, Bournville, Workington and Carnforth. (R.S.Carpenter)

71) Although constructed by BR the 16xx series of 0-6-0 Pannier Tanks were very much Great Western in style following the traditions of such a famous company. All seventy units were designed for use on the Western Region, but there were a few raised eyebrows when Nos 1646 and 1649 were drafted to Scotland at 60C Helmsdale for use on the Dornoch branch in February 1957. Back in England, in September 1964, No 1631 simmers in the yard at Lydney depot. (D.K.Jones)

72) Although the ubiquitous LMS Class 3F 'Jinty' 0-6-0 Tanks were seen at work and rest on all regions of British Railways, the bulk were employed on the London Midland Region. They were utilised in the main on light freight and shunting duties and a small number were permanently stationed at Horwich and Crewe Works. On a sunny 1st June 1951, No 47263 (withdrawn in November 1961) is seen out of steam outside the roundhouse at 18D Staveley (Barrow Hill). (N.E.Preedy)

73) Two months before being reallocated to a new home at 81C Southall, work-stained BR Class 9F 2-10-0 No 92246 (88L Cardiff East Dock) speeds past Elmbridge, between Cheltenham and Gloucester, with a mixed freight on 27th September 1963. In its short seven year existence, No 92246, equipped with a double chimney, also worked from the depots at 81A Old Oak Common, 86C Cardiff (Canton), 86E Severn Tunnel Junction and 85B Gloucester (Horton Road). (N.E.Preedy)

74) Bright sunshine heralds the passing of 21A Saltley based LMS Class 6P5F 'Crab' 2-6-0 No 42761 as it hurtles through Barnt Green station and heads for Bromsgrove with a down fitted freight on 20th June 1959. The author commenced his brief railway career (April 1964 to January 1966) here as a signalbox lad - 'happy days'. During 1964 the sidings at Barnt Green were used to house coaching stock which had been put out of business by football hooligans. (R.S.Carpenter)

75) When brand new in May 1951, BR *Britannia* Class 4-6-2 No 70009 *Alfred the Great* was allocated to 32A Norwich on the Eastern Region. The following month it swapped regions and went to the Southern at 70A Nine Elms and is seen in the yard at 5A Crewe (North) on 30th June of the same year, possibly on a visit to the nearby works to cure some teething troubles. Four months later No 70009 was back at Norwich shed where it remained until September 1961. (R.S.Carpenter)

76) With its smokebox door covered in chalk markings, none of which make any sense to the author, locally based GWR 5700 Class 0-6-0PT No 8743 leaks steam in the weed-strewn shed yard at 85B Gloucester (Horton Road) on a grey 1st September 1960. Once of 88B Cardiff East Dock, 87K Swansea (Victoria), 85A Worcester and 85C Hereford, No 8743 had been at Horton Road since February 1959, A final move, in January 1964, took it to 81A Old Oak Common in London. (Mike Wood)

77) With the familiar landmark of the clocktower near Derby Works and shed on the skyline, the footplate crew of elderly former Midland Railway Class 2P 4-4-0 No 40407 smile collectively at the photographer as their charge trundles along light engine on a sunny 6th July 1954. Just visible in the left background is the lengthy lattice-work pedestrian walk-way from Derby station. Withdrawn from Derby in June 1958, No 40407 was unusually cut up at Crewe Works. (R.S.Carpenter)

78) Staying on the subject of Derby, in 1919 the works produced the unique *'Lickey Banker'*, 0-10-0 No 2290 which became BR No 58100. It acquired the nickname *'Big Bertha'* (although some folk referred to it as *'Big Emma'*). On 26th March 1949 it is seen in a siding near Bromsgrove station whilst awaiting its next call to duty up the incline. Note the electric headlight atop the smokebox door. *'Big Bertha'* was condemned in 1956 after thirty-six years of service. (A.N.H.Glover)

79) It is almost the end of the road for 81E Didcot based GWR 6100 Class 2-6-2T No 6109 as it stands in light steam in the yard at 81F Oxford on 22nd June 1962. Withdrawn the following month, No 6109 was scrapped at King's, Norwich in November 1963. Next to No 6109 is GWR Castle Class 4-6-0 No 7021 *Haverfordwest Castle*, from 81A Old Oak Common. In the background is BR Class 4 4-6-0 No 75022, a local inmate, which survived in service until December 1965. (J.Schatz)

80) Looking rather forlorn, former London & North Western Railway Class 7F 0-8-0 No 49078 stands out of steam in the yard at 21B Bescot on 21st January 1962. Based at Bescot shed since April 1961, No 49078 was drafted south to 1E Bletchley a month after this picture was taken. Condemned in December 1962 it was stored at Nuneaton shed until around October 1964 before being scrapped at Looms, Spondon. In the right of the frame is LMS Class 5 4-6-0 No 44875. (P.A.Rowlings)

81) Paired with a straight-sided tender, GWR *Modified Hall* Class 4-6-0 No 7913 *Little Wyrley Hall*, of 84E Tyseley, heads an express at Hereford station in the mid-fifties. *Little Wyrley Hall* moved on to pastures new at 82B St.Philip's Marsh in May 1958. Prior to withdrawal in March 1965 it also worked from the sheds at Cardiff (Canton), Cardiff East Dock, Neath and Severn Tunnel Junction. It was scrapped at Birds, Bynea in South Wales in July 1965. (R.S.Carpenter)

82) Staveley GC shed, coded 38D and 41H under BR, was a five-minute walk from the Central station until it closed during 1963. It was home to a number of freight orientated locomotive classes including the former GCR O4 Class 2-8-0's and J11 Class 0-6-0's of which Nos 63706 and 64384 are seen in the yard on 13th April 1958. Between December 1962 and March 1964 three condemned LMS *Jubilee* Class 4-6-0's were stored here, these being Nos 45576, 45683 and 45725. (N.E.Preedy)

46

83) Sporting a 'speckled' smokebox door, LMS Class 8F 2-8-0 No 48370, from 16A Nottingham, hurries along near to Tamworth (High Level) with a Birmingham bound freight on 19th April 1963. The driver is looking back from the cab of his charge as he eyes-up three suspicious-looking lads who are 'lurking' by a pillar of the road bridge in the background. No 48370 (withdrawn in November 1966) took its leave of Nottingham shed in May 1964, moving to 16C Derby. (T.R.Amos)

84) Long before the ugly overhead electrification gantries and wires bespoiled the railway scene at Crewe, LMS Unrebuilt *Patriot* Class 4-6-0 No 45503 *The Royal Leicestershire Regiment*, locally based at the North shed (5A), departs from the station with an express on a warm-looking 9th May 1954. No 45503 was transferred to the Midland Division at 26A Newton Heath in July 1958, but returned to 5A three months later. It was withdrawn from service in August 1961. (B.K.B.Green)

85) Fully coaled and ready for its next duty, former Midland Railway Class 3F 0-6-0 No 43832 is hemmed between two other steam locomotives in the yard of its home shed at 18A Toton on 8th June 1958. Of the original series of this particular class, Nos 43775-43833, at this particular date in time there were three other examples of the same stationed at Toton - Nos 43793, 43823 and 43826. All four were drafted away or withdrawn from 18A by November 1959. (B.K.B.Green)

86) GWR *Hall* Class 4-6-0 No 5932 *Haydon Hall* (81A Old Oak Common) and a GWR *Modified Hall* Class 4-6-0 are paired together in the yard at 84A Wolverhampton (Stafford Road) on 30th June 1957. In the right of the frame is the main line from Low Level (GWR) to Shrewsbury and in the background is the lofty viaduct from High Level (LNWR) to Stafford. A vivid memory of the author is walking along canal towpaths to the shed, the canals of which smelt like 'Marmite'! (J.D.Gomersall)

87) BR Class 4 4-6-0 No 75061, of 15C Leicester (Midland), throws up a pall of black smoke as it heads south from Rugby (Midland) with a parcels train on 24th January 1962. No 75061 had been a resident of Leicester (Midland) shed since new in April 1957. It remained there until September 1962, moving to 17A Derby and was withdrawn from 8L Aintree after less than ten years of service. In the background is the local shed's coaling tower and Testing Station. (D.K.Jones)

88) 'Westernised' LMS Class 8F 2-8-0 No 48402, a resident of 2B Oxley since a move from 2C Stourbridge in December 1965, passes through Priestfield station under caution with a partially fitted freight on 20th April 1966. Although having been firmly in the grip of the LMR authorities for a number of years, Priestfield station still retained its GWR lower quadrant signals. It closed during 1972 some five years after No 48402 had been taken out of service. (T.R.Amos)

89) A small group of spotters at Birmingham's Snow Hill station admire the presence of GWR *Grange* Class 4-6-0 No 6833 *Calcot Grange*, from 84B Oxley, which is powering a return excursion from Hastings consisting of Southern Region stock in July 1962. A once longstanding resident of 82B St.Philip's Marsh, No 6833 had spells at Cardiff (Canton) and Penzance sheds before arriving at Oxley in May 1962. Withdrawn in October 1965, it was scrapped during 1966. (R.S.Carpenter)

90) Coupled in front of a begrimed member of the GWR 4300 Class 2-6-0's, BR Class 3 2-6-2T No 82043 is far from its home base at 82E Bristol Barrow Road as it visits 89A Shrewsbury on 22nd October 1962. Once of 88C Barry, No 82043 had been in the Bristol area since June 1958, firstly at 82A Bath Road and then at Barrow Road. Except for a brief spell at 83B Taunton in early 1962 it remained in Bristol until condemned from Barrow Road in February 1964. (N.E.Preedy)

91) Looking fresh from overhaul, LMS Class 6P5F 'Crab' 2-6-0 No 42767 is in the company of sister engine No 42824 (fitted with Reidinger poppet valve gear in 1953) in the yard of their home shed at 17B Burton in February 1957. Whilst No 42767 took its leave of Burton shed in May 1959, going to 9G Gorton, No 42824 stayed on until condemned in July 1962. No 42767 survived at Gorton until March 1963, after which it was cut up at Horwich Works. (N.E.Preedy)

92) With a plethora of various signal designs in the background, LMS *Jubilee* Class 4-6-0 No 45616 *Malta G.C.*, from 14B Kentish Town and paired with a Fowler tender, passes Trent Station North signalbox and rattles over pointwork as it heads an express on 19th August 1951. Drafted to 16A Nottingham in January 1960, *Malta G.C.* also had spells at 15C Leicester (Midland) and 9E Trafford Park before becoming an early victim of modernisation in January 1961. (B.K.B.Green)

93) Steam leaks from the front end of 21B Bescot allocated former London & North Western Railway 7F Class 0-8-0 No 49361 (paired with a tender cab) as it stands near to Wednesbury No. 1 signalbox (LNWR) in 1961. Originally designated as G2 Class locomotives the 460 units were free steaming, powerful and gave little trouble. Between November 1962 and withdrawal in December 1964, No 49361 worked from 21C Bushbury, 5B Crewe (South) and Bescot (twice). (R.S.Carpenter)

94) Locally based LMS *Jubilee* Class 4-6-0 No 45585 *Hyderabad* is smartly turned out as it rests near the open turntable at 17A Derby on 11th May 1952. Another local engine, ex. Midland Railway Class 3F 0-6-0 No 43763, is in the background. *Hyderabad* was transferred from Derby to 14B Kentish Town in July 1957, but returned to the former for a final stint in January 1963 after working from several sheds in the Midland Division and briefly at 14D Neasden. (B.K.B.Green)

95) The Deeley designed (1907) Class 0F 0-4-0 Tanks Nos 41528-41537 were still in situ as a class until mid-1957 when Nos 41530 and 41534 were withdrawn from 22B Gloucester (Barnwood) and 17A Derby respectively. There were no further condemnations until 1961 and two members, Nos 41528 and 41533, were destined to survive in service as late as December 1966 from 41E Staveley Barrow Hill. On 23rd April 1957, No 41529 is parked in the yard at Barrow Hill. (J.D.Gomersall)

96) During the final years of steam at Bromsgrove shed the mainstay of banking duties up the formidable Lickey Incline were examples from the robust GWR 9400 Class 0-6-0 Pannier Tanks. On 1st June 1959 two members of the class, one of them being No 8402, bank a freight train out of Bromsgrove as they tackle the long climb to Blackwell. After the closure of Bromsgrove shed to steam in October 1964, No 8402 was transferred to 85B Gloucester (Horton Road). (D.K.Jones)

97) Bereft of name and cabside numberplates and looking a sorry sight in its uncared for external condition, GWR *Manor* Class 4-6-0 No 7820 *Dinmore Manor* (2B Oxley) defiantly blows off steam as it battles up Danzey bank on the North Warwickshire line with a partially fitted freight in the summer of 1965. Working throughout 1965 from his signalbox at Earlswood Lakes, the author witnessed at first hand the rapid decline of steam power on this route. (R.S.Carpenter)

98) With one of its cylinder cocks open, locally shedded LMS Class 3 2-6-2T No 40173 awaits departure from a weed-strewn siding at Walsall with a pick-up freight in the mid-fifties. With the mass introductions of diesel multiple units and diesel shunters during the late fifties this sturdy class of locomotives was decimated by withdrawals and the class was rendered extinct by December 1962. In July of the same year No 40173 was condemned from 6H Bangor. (R.S.Carpenter)

99) Throughout steam days the extensive and lengthy shed yard at Bescot was noted for its long lines of locomotives, both of the active and stored variety. Today, if travelling on the M6, the lines of steam engines have been replaced by equally long lines of withdrawn and cannibalised diesels - the wheel has turned full circle! In happier days, a former favourite of Oswestry shed, locally based LMS Class 2 2-6-0 No 46527 is noted at 2F on 12th April 1963. (R.S.Carpenter)

100) By Saturday 13th May 1967 steam at 5D Stoke was in its death throes with closure looming within the next three months. Alive in the depot yard over an ash disposal pit is LMS Class 8F 2-8-0 No 48012 and BR Class 4 4-6-0 No 75034, both inmates of Stoke. Shortly before the shed closed to steam both engines had new leases of life at other depots - No 48012 at 8A Edge Hill (Liverpool) and No 75034 at 10A Carnforth. Both engines survived into early 1968. (N.Wood)

101) With a rolling landscape providing a pleasant backdrop, 82C Swindon based GWR *Hall* Class 4-6-0 No 4972 *Saint Brides Hall* approaches Naas Crossing, approximately four miles south of Gloucester, in a flurry of steam and white smoke with a local passenger train in September 1959. A popular resident of Swindon shed for many years, *Saint Brides Hall* lost its regular links with the same when it was transferred to 82D Westbury in July 1962. (A.E.Goulding)

102) A crowded scene in the yard at Westhouses shed, coded 18B and 16G under BR, on a sun-filled summer's day in 1951. Facing the camera is locally based LMS Class 8F 2-8-0 No 48661. Drafted to 16A Toton in January 1961 and 16B Annesley in December 1964, No 48661 found its way back to its former Midland Railway home at Westhouses in June 1965. The reunification was to be all too brief, for it was condemned three months later and cut up at the end of 1965. (R.S.Carpenter)

103) The formation of British Railways meant many lines and stations were duplicated, a situation tolerated until the infamous Doctor Beeching came along. One such location which was to feel the blow of his 'axe' was Gloucester, where Central and Eastgate stations were virtually side by side. One of them had to go and Eastgate eventually closed in 1975. On a misty morning in 1960, Barnwood shed's former MR Class 3F 0-6-0 No 43645 is noted at Eastgate. (R.W.Hinton)

104) Despite the probable presence of more famous locomotives in the yard at 5A Crewe (North), such as LMS *Princess* and *Coronation* Class 4-6-2's, the photographer decided to point his lens at a run-of-the-mill freight locomotive - circa 1952. Paired with an ungainly-looking tender cab, LNWR 7F(G2) Class 0-8-0 No 49410, looking rather smart, is a visitor to 5A from 5C Stafford. Withdrawn from the same in November 1959, No 49410 was scrapped at Crewe Works. (R.S.Carpenter)

105) Once owned by a rival company to the London & North Western Railway, former Midland Railway Class 3F 0-6-0 No 43715, from 19B Sheffield (Grimethorpe), is in light steam facing away from some other 0-6-0 Types at 17A Derby on 1st May 1952. In the right of the frame (background) is a section of Derby Works and nearer to the camera several boilers are scattered on the ground. After condemnation from Grimethorpe in February 1961, No 43715 was also cut up at Crewe. (B.K.B.Green)

106) Introduced into service from 1924 onwards the LMS series of 0-6-0's, Nos 44027-44606, were an updated version of their Midland Railway predecessors, having a power classification of 4F. They were noted on all regions of BR and for the majority of their lives were to be found hauling long rakes of goods wagons. On an unknown date in the fifties, No 44135 (22A Bristol Barrow Road), is observed passing Halesowen Junction with a mixed bag of vehicles. (R.S.Carpenter)

107) A fully laden tender suggests that GWR *Castle* Class 4-6-0 No 5086 *Viscount Horne* is at the start of its journey to Paddington as it heads an express at Cheltenham (Malvern Road) on a sunny 5th June 1949. The real 'Viscount Horne' would not have been too pleased to discover that No 5086 was one of the first examples to be scrapped. Withdrawn from 85A Worcester in November 1958 after completing 1,060,724 miles it was cut up at Swindon Works. (R.S.Carpenter)

108) BR Class 4 4-6-0 No 75053, from 6D Shrewsbury, sports the unusual headcode of 3Z30 to go with its express lamps as it passes through some pleasant scenery near to West Bromwich station on 31st July 1965. No 75053, in charge of an Aberystwyth to Birmingham (Snow Hill) train, had been allocated to the sheds at 6A Chester (twice), 6K Rhyl (twice), 6B Mold Junction, 1E Bletchley, 21D Aston and 5D Stoke before being based at 6D in September 1964. (T.R.Amos)

109) A bright winter's day on 3rd January 1955 reveals the presence of LMS Class 6P5F 'Crab' 2-6-0 No 42831 and BR Class 4 4-6-0 No 75043 in the yard at 15C Leicester (Midland). Extensively rebuilt during 1952 with a new coaling plant and thirty-two road roundhouse, Leicester (Midland) shed lost its links with steam on 13th June 1966. The author happened upon the site by accident during 1997 and all that was left was a few rusting tracks. (B.K.B.Green)

110) Despite being fresh from overhaul, LMS *Jubilee* Class 4-6-0 No 45553 *Canada*, from 9A Longsight (Manchester), looks out of balance with its Fowler tender outside the paint shop at Crewe Works on 14th June 1953. Keeping *Canada* company is another ex.works loco, WD Class 8F 2-8-0 No 90307, of 26B Agecroft, which was destined to die from the same in December 1962. *Canada* fared a little better, being condemned from 5A Crewe (North) in November 1964. (B.K.B.Green)

111) With the sheds at Worcester just visible in the background, locally based GWR *Modified Hall* Class 4-6-0 No 7928 *Wolf Hall* (withdrawn in March 1965) arrives at Shrub Hill station with the four-coach Hereford portion of the 3.10pm express from Worcester to Paddington on 14th March 1963. Although the trackwork has been modified and the steam depot is long gone, Shrub Hill is much the same today as it has always been, complete with semaphore signalling. (J.Schatz)

112) The sun beats down on the railway scene at Gloucester as 83A Newton Abbot based GWR *Castle* Class 4-6-2 No 5024 *Carew Castle* makes its departure from Eastgate station and heads south with *The Cornishman* express from Wolverhampton (Low Level) to Penzance on 25th June 1961. The last time the author saw this loco was at Newton Abbot shed on 29th April 1962, a few days before withdrawal. Scrapping came at the hands of Cashmores, Newport in December 1962. (N.E.Preedy)

113) Accompanied by an 0-6-0 Diesel Shunter, two residents of 41E Staveley (Barrow Hill) seek the sanctuary of their roundhouse on Sunday 25th July 1965. Nearest the camera is LMS Class 0F 0-4-0T No 41528. Tucked behind No 41528 is Kitson designed Class 0F 0-4-0ST No 47001. Both locomotives survived at 41E until December 1966, but for some reason they were stored at 41D Canklow until summoned to Arnott Young's scrapyard at Parkgate and Rawmarsh in 1967. (N.Wood)

114) Today, there is little, if anything, to suggest there was a large steam shed with an extensive layout at the former Great Central Railway owned complex at Annesley on the outskirts of Nottingham. On 25th October 1959 it was still a busy depot with many visitors from other regions, such as LNER B16/1 Class 4-6-0 No 61419 (50A York), seen here in the shed yard. The B16/1 versions, introduced in 1920, were all withdrawn from service by September 1961. (N.E.Preedy)

115) There is an air of decay at Derby (Friargate) on a dull July day in 1965 with weeds taking over the trackwork both in the sidings in the left of the frame and the goods yard to the right as WD Class 8F 2-8-0 No 90295, from 41E Staveley (Barrow Hill), passes through the station with a block oil train. Allocated to 41E from 10F Rose Grove the previous month, No 90295 ended its days of revenue earning service at 40E Colwick, being condemned in January 1966. (N.Wood)

116) Enthusiasts of all ages throng near to a brace of LMS Class 2P 4-4-0's, Nos 40454 (16A Nottingham) and 40489, from 22B Gloucester (Barnwood), during a photo-stop at Cirencester (Watermoor) station with the RCTS 'East Midlander' railtour on 6th May 1956. As the pace of modernisation began to speed up, this was another class to feel the early affects, both being withdrawn during autumn 1960 and scrapped at Gorton and Doncaster Works respectively. (N.E.Preedy)

117) The 'Old Order' at Rugby (Midland) on 21st March 1962, where LMS *Royal Scot* Class 4-6-0 No 46146 *The Rifle Brigade*, an inhabitant of 1A Willesden since a move from 1B Camden in January 1961, departs from the station in a flurry of white smoke with an express. During 1962 no less than thirty-one members of the *Royal Scots* were to disappear from the railway scene for ever, including *The Rifle Brigade* which was condemned from 1A towards the end of the year. (D.K.Jones)

118) Once part of the extensive fleet of BR Class 9F 2-10-0's based at Annesley, No 92089 was drafted to 15C Leicester (Midland) in February 1963. This was followed by a move to 8C Speke Junction in September of the following year. A final transfer in January 1965 took it to 8H Birkenhead. On an unknown date in 1964, No 92089 is noted in the shed yard at 2A Tyseley with a sister locomotive. Withdrawn in February 1967 it was cut up at Drapers, Hull. (D.K.Jones)

119) Following the demise of the mighty GWR *King* Class 4-6-0's from 84A Wolverhampton (Stafford Road) in September 1962, the near-at-hand shed at 84B Oxley began to increase in importance as the former was gradually run-down as a precursor to complete closure a year later. On 7th October 1962 the tracks alongside the running shed at 84B are packed with steam locos, including a visitor from 89A Shrewsbury, GWR *Hall* Class 4-6-0 No 6915 *Mursley Hall*. (J.Schatz)

120) A WD Class 8F 2-8-0 simmers in the background in front of the soot-blackened roundhouse at 16F Burton in August 1965. In the left of the frame is a BR Class 5 4-6-0 whilst the centre of attention for the photographer is BR Class 9F 2-10-0 No 92201 which is a rare visitor to Burton from 36A Doncaster at this stage in time. Equipped with a double chimney, No 92201 commenced its working life at Doncaster in December 1958, but was doomed to die in March 1966. (Ken Ellis)

121) A panoramic view of Worcester during the summer service of 1960 where BR Class 9F 2-10-0 No 92078, of 18A Toton, has been pressed into service on a Saturdays Only stopping train bound for the West of England. To the left of No 92078 a GWR *Hall* Class 4-6-0 gets a freight under way. Constructed by March 1956, No 92078 was allocated to Toton shed from new and remained on its books until transferred to 8B Warrington in March 1965, being withdrawn in May 1967. (N.E.Preedy)

122) The Tewkesbury branch train, consisting of a solitary coach hauled by Class 3F 0-6-0 No 43754, stands in the Malvern line platform at Ashchurch on 2nd June 1961. By this date the service on this line ran no further than Upton-on-Severn and by August 1962 was a thing of the past. Except for the signals this scene is full of Midland Railway interest. Condemned from 85C Gloucester (Barnwood) in October 1962, No 43754 was scrapped at Derby Works. (Peter Hay)

123) GWR *Castle* Class 4-6-0 No 5089 *Westminster Abbey*, from 84A Wolverhampton (Stafford Road), leaves Gloucester (Eastgate) with a Wolverhampton (Low Level) to Paignton express on 18th June 1962. Today, all that remains of this scene is the public house in the left of the picture and the retaining wall on which the photographer stood. Reallocated to 84B Oxley in September 1963 following the closure of the latter, No 5089 survived until November 1964. (N.E.Preedy)

124) Under threat of replacement by the newly constructed *Western* Diesel-Hydraulics, GWR *King* Class 4-6-0 No 6005 *King George II*, of 81A Old Oak Common, barks defiantly as it blasts up Hatton bank with the 4.10pm express from Paddington to Birkenhead on Whit Monday 1962. A regular inmate of 84A Stafford Road, *King George II* had been moved to Old Oak in September 1961. After withdrawal in November 1962 it was disposed of by Cashmores, Great Bridge. (P.A.Bridgman)

125) A crowded depot yard at Coalville, coded 17C, 15D and 15E under BR, on 8th July 1951. Nearest the camera is a local inmate in the shape of LMS Class 3F 0-6-0 No 43682. Behind No 43682 is LMS Class 8F 2-8-0 No 48378, from 15A Wellingborough. Also in the frame is LMS Class 4F 0-6-0 No 43835, of Coalville. Later in life No 43682 ended up on the former Somerset & Dorset Joint Railway at 71J Highbridge and 82G Templecombe, being withdrawn in September 1962. (B.K.B.Green)

126) By January 1957 the vast majority of the surviving Johnson Midland Railway Class 2F 0-6-0's, first introduced in 1875, were based at many depots on the London Midland Region, including 18A Toton, where one example, No 58173, is seen out of steam in June 1959. Used mainly for light freight and shunting duties, two members of the class, Nos 58148 and 58182 survived until January 1964. After condemnation in June 1960, No 58173 was scrapped at Gorton Works. (N.E.Preedy)

127) Under leaden skies, GWR Churchward heavy freight locomotive 2800 Class 2-8-0 No 2867, from 86G Pontypool Road, gets a Gloucester bound freight on the move from Worcester (Shrub Hill) on 5th August 1960. Once of 81D Reading, No 2867 moved to South Wales in October 1957, firstly to 86C Cardiff (Canton) and then to 86E Severn Tunnel Junction in February 1959. It remained in South Wales until withdrawal from 86A Newport (Ebbw Junction) in July 1963. (N.E.Preedy)

128) On a bright 9th August 1964 at 16D Nottingham, LMS Class 5 4-6-0 No 45221, a recent transfer to the depot from 16C Derby, stands out of steam on a back road near to the roundhouses. Shortly before the closure of the shed to steam, No 45221 was reallocated to 8F Springs Branch Wigan in March 1965. Nottingham shed's most famous inmate was the pioneer LMS *Royal Scot* Class 4-6-0 No 46100 which was withdrawn for preservation from the same in October 1962. (N.E.Preedy)

129) GWR 4300 Class 2-6-0 No 5336, seen in steam near to the coaling stage at 89A Shrewsbury, is far from its home base at 86E Severn Tunnel Junction on a misty 17th June 1961. A former inmate of the sheds at 83D Laira (Plymouth) and St.Philip's Marsh, No 5336 was allocated to Severn Tunnel Junction in February 1959. In October 1963 it was transferred to 83B Taunton for use on the picturesque line to Barnstaple which was a bastion of steam until September 1964. (D.K.Jones)

130) LMS *Royal Scot* Class 4-6-0 No 46162 *Queen's Westminster Rifleman* (1B Camden) emerges from beneath the flyover from Northampton as it heads south towards London (Euston) after departing from Rugby (Midland) with an up express in October 1959. The following month *Queen's Westminster Rifleman* took its leave of Camden, moving to the Midland Division at 14B Kentish Town. Its final home was at 12A Carlisle (Kingmoor), being withdrawn in June 1964. (D.K.Jones)

131) With a smoke-blackened awning for company, BR Class 5 4-6-0 No 73093, from 84G Shrewsbury, lifts its safety valves whilst in charge of a local passenger train at Stafford in October 1958. Transferred to Shrewsbury the previous month from 10C Patricroft, No 73093 remained on the WR until April 1965, also serving from the sheds at Barnwood and Horton Road in Gloucester and Bath Green Park. Its final allocations were at 70D Eastleigh and 70C Guildford. (R.S.Carpenter)

132) Coupled to an unidentified sister locomotive, GWR 5700 Class 0-6-0PT No 8792 still carries its previous owner's initials on its panniers despite in excess of ten years having passed by since nationalisation. No 8792 is pictured here in front of the roundhouse at its home shed of 84F Stourbridge on a sunny 15th April 1958. It remained on the books at Stourbridge until condemned in February 1962, being scrapped at Cashmores, Newport three months later. (N.E.Preedy)

133) A trio of engines are bathed in warm sunshine in the yard at 3A Bescot in July 1956. Leading the line-up is ex.works LMS Class 6P5F 'Crab' 2-6-0 No 42782, from 3D Aston, behind which is an LMS *Jubilee* Class 4-6-0 and a former LNWR Class 7F 0-8-0. Between February 1957 and March 1963, No 42782 was based at Bescot itself, Crewe (South), Rugby, Aston (again) and Stoke. For a brief period of time, March to October 1963, it was shedded at 67C Ayr. (N.E.Preedy)

134) Highly polished former Midland Railway Class 3F 0-6-0 No 43618, from far-off 8B Warrington, is employed on a joint SLS/MLS railtour of the High Peak lines and is noted in the middle of nowhere at Ludmanlow during a photo-stop on 25th April 1953. No 43618 remained at Warrington until February 1957 after which it was subjected to a flurry of transfers, firstly to 2B Nuneaton, then to 11B Barrow and finally to 6K Rhyl where it was to die in March 1962. (B.K.B.Green)

135) Released into traffic at Preston shed from new in September 1954, BR Class 2 2-6-0 No 78030 found itself on the books at 5A Crewe (North) from April 1956. It was destined to remain at the depot until October 1964, being despatched 'up the road' to 5B Crewe (South). On 20th October 1963 it looks in fine external fettle in the yard at 5A. Condemned from Crewe (South) shed in October 1965, No 78030 was briefly stored at Crewe Works prior to scrapping. (D.K.Jones)

136) Its lined paintwork gleaming in bright sunshine, LMS Class 4P 'Compound' 4-4-0 No 40933, from 3E Monument Lane in Birmingham, proudly waits to be steamed again after overhaul at Derby Works on 14th October 1951. Also present is LMS Stanier 3-cylinder Class 4 2-6-4T No 42532, from 33C Shoeburyness on the Eastern Region. In December 1957, No 40933 was drafted to the North Eastern Region at 55E Normanton, but was condemned from there in April 1958. (B.K.B.Green)

137) By the autumn of 1965 steam workings from the Toton area of Nottingham were rapidly becoming a thing of the past. With the old depot in the background virtually redundant it was left to other depots to provide power for the dwindling number of rostered steam powered trains. In this picture 15A Leicester (Midland) has provided LMS Class 8F 2-8-0 No 48698 to head a lengthy rake of mineral wagons. It was withdrawn from 16B Colwick in April 1966. (N.Wood)

138) Despite the abolition of the steam locomotive in normal everyday service and the sweeping away of the old semaphore signals and signalboxes, little has changed at Tyseley over the years. It remains as a junction for the North Warwickshire line and the station is still in situ thanks to its status as a listed building. In earlier times, GWR *Modified Hall* Class 4-6-0 No 7915 *Mere Hall*, of 84B Oxley, steams into platform one with an up local in 1956. (D.K.Jones)

139) With a partially clear road ahead, LMS Class 5 4-6-0 No 45205, from 24B Rose Grove, steams alongside some duckboards at Rugby (Midland) with a fitted freight in the late fifties. Designed by Stanier, No 45205, withdrawn from 9D Newton Heath in October 1966, was built at the Armstrong Whitworth factory in 1935 and is seen here with a domeless boiler. In the left of the frame, LMS *Coronation* Class 4-6-2 No 46228 *Duchess of Rutland* heads a parcels train. (R.S.Carpenter)

140) A rather less than clean GWR *Grange* Class 4-6-0, No 6854 *Roundhill Grange*, shedded at 84E Tyseley, simmers patiently in Shrewsbury station with a passenger train on 16th June 1962. Despite Nos 6801, 6802 and 6805 being condemned in 1960 and 1961, the *Granges* remained virtually unscathed during the mass steam withdrawals of 1962, No 6865 being the only victim and by January 1965, their last year of service, some forty-five examples were still active. (D.K.Jones)

141) Four lifeless locomotives are sidelined at 5B Crewe (South) on 6th September 1961. Leading the line is 8B Warrington based LMS Unrebuilt *Patriot* Class 4-6-0 No 45550. Bringing up the rear is an LMS Class 4 2-6-4T, an LMS *Jubilee* Class 4-6-0 and a BR Class 9F 2-10-0. Later serving from the sheds at Lancaster (Green Ayre) and Carnforth, No 45550 was withdrawn from the latter in November 1962. After a lengthy period of storage it was cut up at Crewe Works. (R.W.Hinton)

142) Bereft of tender, BR Class 4 4-6-0 No 75029 stands amidst the weeds at 2D Banbury on 31st May 1964. Constructed by May 1954, No 75029 had a short but distinguished career based from the sheds at Laira (Plymouth), Oxford, Gloucester (Horton Road), Southport, Swindon, Tyseley, Machynlleth, Croes Newydd, Llandudno Junction and Stoke before being withdrawn from the latter in August 1967. Today, No 75029 is actively preserved on the East Somerset Railway. (Terry Ward)

143) Hemmed between two locomotives, May 1949 built GWR *Castle* Class 4-6-0 No 7018 *Drysllwyn Castle* is a visitor to 81F Oxford from 81A Old Oak Common on 30th June 1962. Famous for its exploits on the *Bristolian* whilst based at 82A Bristol (Bath Road), No 7018 had been an Old Oak Common steed since October 1961. Condemned from 81A in September 1963 after covering only 614,259 miles, *Drysllwyn Castle* was cut up at Cashmores, Great Bridge in 1964. (R.Picton)

144) The driver of BR *Britannia* Class 4-6-2 No 70010 *Owen Glendower* (1A Willesden) appears unperturbed as his charge thunders past a spotter on his haunches under the wires to the south of Crewe in August 1962. *Owen Glendower*, in charge of a Windermere to Euston express, had been at Willesden shed since April of the same year after being transferred from 31B March on the Eastern Region. Constructed by May 1951, No 70010 met its end in September 1967. (Kit Windle)

145) With the young fireman smiling brashly at the camera, nicely turned-out LMS Class 4 2-6-4T No 42552, from 3E Monument Lane, awaits departure from Walsall station with a local passenger turn on a bright day in 1955. These locomotives were a common sight on such workings in the West Midlands until the advent of diesel multiple units. No 42552, drafted to 3D Aston in October 1957, was to fall early victim to modernisation, being condemned in October 1961. (R.S.Carpenter)

146) With an 0-6-0 Diesel Shunter trailing behind, LMS Class 5 4-6-0 No 45350, of 5D Stoke, rolls along at a steady pace with a ballast train at London Road, Derby in the summer of 1966. Once of 1A Willesden, No 45350 was an inmate of Stoke shed from July 1960 until March 1967. During the last seventeen months or so of life, No 45350 served from the depots at 8F Springs Branch Wigan and 10F Rose Grove. Withdrawn in August 1968, it was cut up four months later. (N.Wood)

147) Apart from being posted at a host of sub-sheds all over the BR system, some locomotives, particularly those of the small variety, were seconded on loan to industrial locations. This is the case with former MR Class 1F 0-6-0 No 41844 (16B Kirkby-in-Ashfield) noted in bright sunshine near the NCB shed at Worksop Colliery on 27th July 1963. Although condemned from Kirkby in May 1964, No 41844 was stored at 41E Stavely (Barrow Hill) prior to scrapping. (N.E.Preedy)

148) During 1955, ten members of the BR Class 9F 2-10-0's, Nos 92020-92029, were fitted with Crosti-boilers in an effort to save on coal consumption. These proved to be only minimal and with the chimneys located in front of the right side of the cab they were dirty and objectionable to work with. All were based at 15A Wellingborough and No 92026 is seen at the depot in 1958. Although reverting to 'normal' in later years they retained the Crosti-boilers. (Eric Light)

149) The 120 units of the GWR 2251 Class 0-6-0's were extremely popular and there was hardly a secondary or branch line on the Western Region which was not graced by their presence. On 3rd May 1952, No 2249, from 85C Hereford, simmers in a platform at Gloucester (Central) with a local passenger. Rendered redundant from Hereford shed in June 1963, No 2249 moved to a final home at 81D Reading, being taken out of traffic from the same in September 1964. (N.E.Preedy)

150) Situated on the West Coast Main Line, almost 125 miles from London (Euston), Rugeley (Trent Valley) is the setting for this late 1950's picture. 5B Crewe (South) allocated LMS Class 6P5F 'Crab' 2-6-0 No 42920 rushes through the station with a fitted freight. Reallocated to 3D Aston and 5D Stoke, between September 1958 and February 1960, No 42920 went to 8A Edge Hill (Liverpool) in November 1962. Withdrawn in December 1964 it was scrapped at a local yard. (R.S.Carpenter)

151) Locally based BR *Britannia* Class 4-6-2 No 70031 *Byron* stands in the yard at 21D Aston on a gloomy 17th February 1962. When *Byron* and several sister engines were drafted here in August and September 1961 the local spotters were so excited there was an unprecedented mass invasion of the depot on one particular occasion. However, the local British Transport Police were ready and waiting and had a 'field day' with countless arrests for 'trespass'. (R.S.Carpenter)

152) Paintwork gleaming, LMS *Jubilee* Class 4-6-0 No 45670 *Howard of Effingham*, from 8A Edge Hill (Liverpool), is fresh from overhaul at Crewe Works on 1st April 1951. Records show us that *Howard of Effingham* remained at 8A until June 1960 when it moved to 5A Crewe (North). Further transfers, prior to withdrawal in October 1964, took No 45670 to 1A Willesden, 2A Rugby, 16C Derby and 9B Stockport. It was cut up at Wards, Killamarsh in February 1965. (B.K.B.Green)

153) Despite being high summer it is a wet and miserable day at Gloucester on 17th July 1954. With a GWR 9400 Class 0-6-0PT also in the frame, GWR *Hall* Class 4-6-0 No 5903 *Keele Hall*, allocation not known, awaits departure from Central station with the 2.40pm local to Swindon. From at least January 1957 onwards, *Keele Hall* was based at depots in Wales - 87H Neyland, 87F Llanelly (twice) and 86C/88A Cardiff (Canton). It was condemned from the latter in September 1963. (N.E.Preedy)

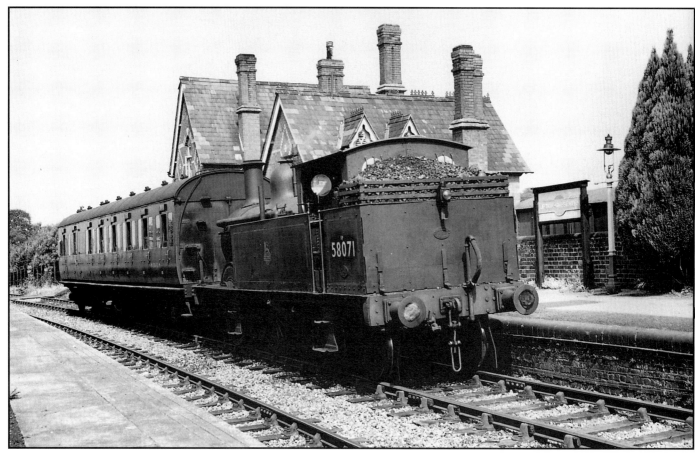

154) This delightful rural scene at Upton-upon-Severn on 27th August 1955 depicts former Midland Railway Class 1P 0-4-4T No 58071 en route between Ashchurch and Malvern. As a single carriage sufficed for the potential travelling public on offer it was hardly surprising that passenger services were withdrawn on 14th August 1961. The locomotive (ex. LMS No 1377), from a class first introduced in 1881, went to its last resting place in July 1956. (A.N.H.Glover)

155) GWR inspired but BR built (June 1949) *Castle* Class 4-6-0 No 7024 *Powis Castle* (81A Old Oak Common) steams into Birmingham (Snow Hill) station with an up empty stock train on 20th May 1959. Surplus to operating requirements at Old Oak Common in September 1961, *Powis Castle* was drafted to 84A Wolverhampton (Stafford Road). Condemned from its final home at 2B Oxley in February 1965, No 7024 was scrapped at Cashmores, Great Bridge four months later. (D.K.Jones)

156) During the late fifties and early sixties, LMS Ivatt Class 2 2-6-2T No 41219 spent most of its time working from Northampton shed, coded 2C, 4B, 2E and 1H under BR. The exceptions were at 6H Bangor, from December 1961 until April 1962, and 15A Leicester (Midland) from July 1965 until withdrawal in October of the same year. During its second spell at Northampton, No 41219 lets off steam in the shed yard on 29th December 1963. The shed closed in September 1965. (Terry Ward)

157) The 'humble' is overshadowed by the 'mighty' in the depot yard at 15A Wellingborough on 13th September 1957, where LMS Class 3 2-6-2T No 40061 (newly allocated to 17E Heaton Mersey) is a visitor as is BR Class 9F 2-10-0 No 92110, from 14A Cricklewood in London. No 40061 had been transferred to the LMR at 1C Watford from 53B Hull (Botanic Gardens) on the NER in March 1957. Withdrawn in December 1959, it was cut up at the Central Wagon Co., Wigan. (B.K.B.Green)

158) With a smart array of lower quadrant signals in the background, a plume of white smoke is thrown high into the Worcestershire sky as GWR *County* Class 4-6-0 No 1013 *County of Dorset* (89A Shrewsbury) accelerates out of Worcester (Shrub Hill) with a Paddington bound express in 1961. Equipped with a double chimney in February 1958, *County of Dorset* made its leave of Shrewsbury shed in September 1963 moving to a final abode at 82C Swindon. (N.E.Preedy)

159) By May 1957, 22B Gloucester (Barnwood) owned two of the diminutive Deeley LMS Class 0F 0-4-0 Tanks, Nos 41535 and 41537. Both were destined to remain at Barnwood until the autumn of 1963. In June 1957, No 41537, looking fresh from shops, is employed at Gloucester Docks Sidings. Adjacent is the now closed Gloucester Railway Carriage and Wagon Works which turned out many items for BR and overseas railways. Today, there is no trace of this little yard. (N.E.Preedy)

160) Although one did not know it at the time the sun was setting on the magnificent LMS *Coronation* Class 4-6-2's as No 46251 *City of Nottingham*, from 5A Crewe (North), heads the RCTS 'East Midlander' bound for Swindon at Nottingham on 9th May 1964. *City of Nottingham* was the last example of the class which the author had the privilege to travel behind in normal service, from Perth to Carlisle on a Sundays Only express to Euston on 2nd August 1964. (N.E.Preedy)

161) A 'stranger-in-the-camp' in the yard at 81F Oxford on 20th May 1956 where 15A Wellingborough based BR Crosti-boilered Class 9F 2-10-0 No 92027 is noted out of steam. Ousted from Wellingborough shed in January 1964 by diesel traction, No 92027 moved the short distance to 15C Kettering. Its last abode was at 8H Birkenhead, from November 1964 up until withdrawal in August 1967, after which it was cut up at Buttigiegs, Newport at the end of the year. (R.S.Carpenter)

162) With a host of steam locomotives in the background where we can also make out the covered southern roundhouse, begrimed former Midland Railway Class 3F 0-6-0 No 43242 is on its own in a siding at 21A Saltley on a February day in 1960. Once of 16B Kirkby-in-Ashfield, No 43242 had been at Saltley shed since January 1959. Employed in the main on light freight work, this engine could often be seen on banking duties on the Camp Hill avoiding line. (J.James)

163) LMS Class 3 2-6-2T No 40122, from 2B Nuneaton, has been purloined by the shed staff to act as a station pilot at Stafford in February 1957 where it is seen in a bay platform. The author 'discovered' the delights of Stafford as a young lad whilst on a holiday trip from Birmingham to Rhyl in May 1957, 'copping' LMS *Royal Scot* Class 4-6-0 No 46161 *King's Own* and LMS *Coronation* Class 4-6-2 No 46253 *City of St.Albans* in a matter of a couple of minutes. (R.S.Carpenter)

164) 84A Wolverhampton (Stafford Road) only ever had a small number of the GWR 9400 Class 0-6-0 Pannier Tanks on its books at any one time and one example, No 8452, in fine external fettle, moves the stock of an auto-train at Wolverhampton (Low Level) on 25th August 1960. Once of 84C Banbury and 85A Worcester, No 8452 moved to 88L Cardiff East Dock in December 1952. Condemned from the latter in April 1964 it was scrapped at Swindon Works four months later. (D.K.Jones)

165) Stripped of boiler cladding, three LMS Class 4P 'Compound' 4-4-0's, including Nos 41014 and 41035, await attention in the yard at Derby Works on 11th May 1952. Also awaiting attention is LMS Stanier 3-cylinder Class 4 2-6-4T No 42535, from 33C Shoeburyness. During 1957 and 1958 the 'Compounds' were decimated by withdrawals and by January 1959 only nineteen examples remained in stock. The last survivor, No 41168, was condemned in July 1961. (B.K.B.Green)

166) With the high level line from Birmingham to Derby just visible in the background, LMS *Royal Scot* Class 4-6-0 No 46135 *The East Lancashire Regiment*, of 9A Longsight (Manchester), storms southwards through Lichfield (Trent Valley) with a Manchester (London Road) to Euston express in June 1955. After two spells at 5A Crewe (North), one at 1B Camden and a further stint at Longsight, No 46135 was drafted to 55A Leeds (Holbeck) in August 1962. (D.K.Jones)

167) Begrimed GWR *Castle* Class 4-6-0 No 7013 *Bristol Castle* (2A Tyseley) takes the Western Region tracks towards Stroud at Standish Junction on 3rd October 1964 with a partially fitted freight bound for Acton goods yard. All is not as it seems for No 7013 was in fact No 4082 *Windsor Castle* which swopped identities with the original No 7013 for the funeral of King George VI on 15th February 1952 and the identities never changed back again. (N.E.Preedy)

168) Many types of locomotives were overhauled at Crewe Works and even unsung heavy freight types could be made to look special as is the case with WD Class 8F 2-8-0 No 90266, from 24C Lostock Hall, seen in the Works yard on 13th October 1957. No 90266 also worked from 24B Rose Grove and 9G Gorton before being transferred to the Eastern Region in September 1964. Allocated to Langwith Junction and Staveley GC/Barrow Hill sheds it was withdrawn in July 1965. (N.E.Preedy)

169) LMS Class 5 4-6-0 No 44813 (21A Saltley) battles its way up the 1 in 37 gradient of the Lickey Incline near to Burcot, between Bromsgrove and Blackwell, assisted in the rear by GWR 9400 Class 0-6-0 Pannier Tanks Nos 8402 and 8406 with a northbound express on 25th July 1959. A re-enactment of this once common sight was witnessed by hundreds of people when LMS Class 6P5F No 2968 and GWR 4300 Class 2-6-0 No 7325 were utilised on 22nd November 1997. (A.N.H.Glover)

170) With a clear road ahead, GWR *Modified Hall* Class 4-6-0 No 6964 *Thornbridge Hall*, from the nearby local shed, departs from Shrewsbury with a passenger working on a dull 3rd June 1961. *Thornbridge Hall* had been a Shrewsbury engine since moving from 84A Wolverhampton (Stafford Road) in July 1957. It took its leave of the shed in November 1964, moving to 2A Tyseley. Withdrawn from a final abode at 2D Banbury, No 6964 was scrapped at Wards, Beighton, Sheffield. (D.K.Jones)

171) The Unrebuilt *Patriot* Class 4-6-0's were the first passenger engines on the LMR to be affected by withdrawals when the main line diesel invasion started and a number were stored at 2A Rugby for many months before being called to the scrapyard, these being Nos 45537, 45538, 45541, 45542, 45544 and 45548. No 45538 *Giggleswick* (2B Nuneaton) is noted at Rugby with a sacked chimney on 13th May 1962, four months before being officially taken out of service. (P.A.Rowlings)

172) 'Mother Nature' is beginning to reclaim the yard at 85B Gloucester (Horton Road) on a misty 1st September 1962. Neglected by the cleaning staff at 82E Bristol Barrow Road, GWR *Grange* Class 4-6-0 No 6860 *Aberporth Grange* is a visitor to the shed. Several other locomotives are scattered about, including locally based GWR 5700 Class 0-6-0PT No 8743, seen in the right of the frame. *Aberporth Grange* was withdrawn from 88L Cardiff East Dock in February 1965. (Mike Wood)

173) Despite looking in good condition there is only five months of life ahead for GWR 4300 Class 2-6-0 No 7327, of 81E Didcot, as it passes beneath a broad-spanned signal gantry on a through road at Oxford with a southbound Class 8 loose-coupled freight in June 1964. Once of 81C Southall, No 7327 had been a Didcot steed since September 1958. Originally numbered 9305 it became No 7327 in January 1959 and after withdrawal it was cut up at Swindon Works. (I.J.Hodson)

174) Still bearing the logo of its former master on its tender, LMS Class 4F 0-6-0 No 44110 is a visitor to 21A Saltley from 16B Peterborough (Spital Bridge) on 13th August 1949. This locomotive remained at Spital Bridge even after it was taken over by the Eastern Region on 1st February 1958 not leaving until the shed closed in February 1960. It later served from the depots at Northampton (twice), Nuneaton, Bescot, Aston, Springs Branch Wigan and Buxton. (A.N.H.Glover)